GREAT CAREERS IN THE SPORTS INDUSTRY™

A DREAM JOB AS A SPORTS AGENT

MARY-LANE KAMBERG

Rosen YA™
New York

For Mary Ladewig

Published in 2018 by The Rosen Publishing Group, Inc.
29 East 21st Street, New York, NY 10010

First Edition

Library of Congress Cataloging-in-Publication Data

Names: Kamberg, Mary-Lane, 1948– author.
Title: A dream job as a sports agent / Mary-Lane Kamberg.
Description: New York : Rosen Publishing, 2018 | Series: Great careers in the sports industry | Includes bibliographical references and index. | Audience: Grades 7–12.
Identifiers: LCCN 2017013853 | ISBN 9781538381366 (library bound) | ISBN 9781508178606 (paperback)
Subjects: LCSH: Sports agents—Juvenile literature. | Sports—Vocational guidance—Juvenile literature.
Classification: LCC GV734.5 .K36 2018 | DDC 796.023—dc23
LC record available at https://lccn.loc.gov/2017013853

Manufactured in China

CONTENTS

INTRODUCTION

The business of professional sports relies on more than the game itself. Behind the scenes, sports agents guide athletes' careers from the draft to post-season careers.

It's game day in the exciting world of high school and college sports. Some individuals are on the field, performing skills they've trained for years to perfect. Others fill the seats in the stands as passionate fans. Some of the players will move on to professional teams. And some of the fans will go into the industry of professional sports as important movers and shakers behind the scenes, helping athletes achieve their lifelong dreams.

A sports agent is the middleman—or woman—who helps players connect with professional teams. He or she not only negotiates contracts, but also manages the athlete's money, image, and—in some cases—nearly every aspect of the player's personal and professional life. It's a fulfilling, frustrating, frenzied occupation. The job is also lots of fun for those who love the fast-paced drama of the world of sports.

A career as a sports agent is not for the faint of heart. It's hectic and highly competitive. It takes a significant amount of preparation that can start as early as high school classes and extracurricular activities. A bachelor's degree from an accredited college or university is a bare minimum level of education. Most agents have a master's degree in business administration or sports management or a law degree specializing in sports law.

In addition to formal education, sports agents need a connection to sports. Some were athletes themselves. Perhaps they worked as instructors at sports camps or caddied at a golf course. Friendships with other players, as well as coaches and other individuals in the sports industry, can pay off by providing leads to potential clients. If not a player, a sports agent candidate needs experience in such areas as marketing, event planning, sales, or some other environment that offers exposure to the business of college or professional sports. Perhaps he or she worked in a college athletic ticket office or interned with a television station.

In addition to having a degree, a sports agent must be certified by the players associations of different sports. Certification includes attending informational seminars and passing a test that covers collective bargaining agreements, players association regulations, policies about substance abuse and performance-enhancing drugs, and other issues.

Then there are fees to take the exams, league dues, and professional liability insurance premiums. A newbie sports agent also needs a healthy bank account to pay for personal expenses, as well as travel, meals, lodging, and training for clients before anyone signs an income-producing contract with a professional team.

Seasoned sports agents recommend that someone new to the occupation start as an employee at an established sports agency or management company that has plenty of clients. Like all job seekers, applicants need an impressive (but truthful) **résumé** and a list of places to apply. They need to practice interview skills to get ready for job interviews by conveying a confident—but not cocky—attitude and professional approach to the work.

Once on the job, a sports agent can never stand still. He or she must stay in motion, keeping track of trends and changing laws and regulations, looking for talented athletes with promise, and serving current clients, all while constantly networking. Read on to see if a career as a sports agent is right for you.

Chapter 1 A DAY IN THE LIFE

It's a Sunday in April, the second day of the National Football League (NFL) draft, and John is busy. As the sports agent for three college football players, he hopes they'll all get a shot at turning pro. None were taken in the first three rounds, but today the wide receiver, punter, and offensive lineman will have chances in four more rounds of thirty-two picks for each NFL team.

Armed with a smartphone that contains more than seven thousand contact numbers, John attends a draft-day party at the home of his wide receiver. The player is surrounded by family and friends all glued to the television screen. But John can't spend much time in the living room. He's outside sending text messages and emails about all of his clients to scouts, team executives, and general managers, and he is receiving calls and callbacks from team representatives.

John's punter gets an offer for a tryout, but John wants him to hold out for a roster spot. The punter goes

Like most sports agents, Scott Boras spends a lot of time on his phone serving clients, contacting potential players, and speaking with team representatives.

in the fourth round, and John immediately phones to congratulate him. In the middle of the call, a scout from another team beeps in to talk about the wide receiver in the living room. John asks about the team's possible need for an offensive linebacker, his other client who hasn't been drafted yet.

The phone rings with an offer for the linebacker. John calls the player, who accepts. As the seventh and last round begins, John goes supersonic in a flurry of phone calls and texts. Three teams seem interested in the wide receiver, and John knows his player has a favorite among them. While John is talking to a different team, the phone rings in the living room. The head coach of the player's most-wanted team calls the player directly. After consulting with John, the player accepts the offer.

It's been a frantic, stress-filled day, but John's work is not over. In the next days he will be responsible for negotiating each player's contract, based on the team offers and what John estimates each player's value to his team should be. And soon John will continue to build the intimate relationship that exists between professional athlete and their agent.

WHAT SPORTS AGENTS DO

Sports agents are also known as sports brokers, player agents, and player negotiators. They are legal representatives for professional athletes and others involved in the business side of sports as managers and coaches. Agents' main responsibility is to negotiate contracts for their clients. The contracts include those between players and teams, but also those for endorsements, personal appearances, and other activities. Beyond that, agents work to improve their clients' career prospects—both as active players and in such post-retirement occupations as sports broadcast announcers and commentators or business owners.

But sports agents fill many other roles, as well. They may also act as business and financial managers,

Some retired professional athletes, like Kevin Weekes (*center*) and Michael Ryan Rupp of the National Hockey League, become sports commentators—often with their sports agents' help.

public relations "image makers," amateur doctors who know the difference between minor and career-ending injuries, referral sources to financial experts and medical specialists, and sometimes amateur psychiatrists, mentors, parental figures, and friends.

Agents may be lawyers themselves or recommend legal services when necessary. In every way, sports agents look out for their clients' best interests. That might include giving money-management advice, arranging post-career employment, or running interference with the media if a negative story breaks that affects a player's reputation.

Sports agents work with all types of sports, including golf, football, hockey, ice skating, and basketball. Depending on the sport, they represent eligible college athletes, foreign athletes, and Olympians. They even work for high school athletes in baseball and hockey.

A TYPICAL DAY?

A career as a sports agent is hectic and exciting. Each day is different. On some days agents make travel arrangements to scout new players, attend sports marketing events, or meet with clients or team representatives. On other days, agents travel, often by car. In fact, almost every day involves traffic or the open road.

Sports agents usually have offices at home or at an agency. However, they spend most of their time driving or riding in a car—almost always on the phone.

"I'm driving all the time—to and from the office, to and from the airport or hotel or meeting," David Canter told ESPN.com. Canter is a certified NFL sports agent and president and founder of Total Entertainer

SHOWING OFF SKILLS

Agents are always looking for potential new clients. One way to find them is to attend showcase events and tournaments. For example, the NFL Scouting Combine is a week-long event held in February or March. Players perform mental and physical drills, tests, and evaluations that demonstrate their size, speed, and strength. Their physical measurements are recorded, and their joint movement is evaluated. The activities include:

- *Forty-yard dash*
- *Shuttle drills (for quickness and changing direction)*
- *Vertical jump*
- *Broad jump*
- *Personal interviews*
- *A fifty-question Wonderlic intelligence test*
- *Drug screening*

The combine gives invited college football players a chance to be seen—and hopefully noticed—by scouts, coaches, and general managers. After the combine, agents talk to team representatives about their potential and current clients' performances.

and Athlete Management. "And I'm always on the phone. On a typical day, I'm in on three hundred to five hundred phone calls—up to three hundred outgoing, two hundred incoming. My cell phone is always on. I sleep with it at night. I'm never surprised when the phone rings at 3:00 a.m. Sometimes it's a call from clients. Sometimes it's from clients' wives. Sometimes it's from clients' girlfriends asking where their boyfriends are."

Agents need to stay in touch with their clients—perhaps phoning each one several times a week. They also check in with teams' general managers to discuss present or future needs. Agents can expect contacts from sports organizations any time—day or night, weekdays or weekends.

Agents handle hundreds of requests from businesses asking players to endorse products or services. The agents must sort through the offers, keeping each player's image in mind and recommending which businesses support that image. Agents then negotiate contracts for the deals.

Being an NFL agent, for example, is a 24-hour, 365-days-a-year job. On Sundays during football season, agents take in as many as seven games at once. But they're not relaxing and eating pizza with friends. They're looking for opportunities for their clients. A

Sports agents represent Olympians, negotiating contracts for endorsements, personal appearances, broadcasting, and other opportunities. The agents must be aware of eligibility rules as well as substance abuse regulations.

missed field goal after a series of bad kicks by the same player can mean a tryout for the errant kicker's position for an out-of-work placekicker looking for a job. And the kicker's agent likely has the team's director of player personnel on the phone before the end of the quarter.

SHOW ME THE MONEY

Being a sports agent can be a fun career. An agent is always in the action, hanging out with sports superstars, coaches, and other team professionals. Agents enjoy helping athletes reach their lifelong goals.

The career can be financially rewarding, as

well. Agents charge clients in different ways. They might get a percentage of the athlete's contract. The amount ranges from 3 percent to 10 percent of the player's salary, depending on the sport. Although Major League Baseball (MLB) and the National Hockey League (NHL) have no limits on an agent's commission, both the NFL and National Basketball Association (NBA) players associations cap the commission at 3 percent, according to the *Houston Chronicle* in 2017.

Agents also cash in on endorsements they negotiate for their athletes, earning between 10 percent and 20 percent, depending on the sport and product or service endorsed. Agents for track and field stars, for example, get 15 percent of shoe contracts and 20 percent of everything else they arrange. Commissions for personal appearances also range between 10 percent and 20 percent, all according to the *Houston Chronicle*.

Some agents charge a flat fee or by the hour. Or, agents might base compensation on a combination of two or more of these methods. Total agent earnings depend on the talent and performance of the athletes they represent, as well as the number of clients.

Successful agents who represent top athletes can make more than $1 million per year, according to Become-a-Sports-Agent.com. Really successful ones make even more. However, not all agents represent top athletes. Earnings for most agents are often quite a bit less.

TOP FIVE MOST VALUABLE SPORTS AGENCIES

Based on the value of contracts negotiated and managed, Forbes ranked the following sports agencies as the top five in the world in 2016:

Creative Artists Agency (CAA) dominates the sports agency industry. Its NFL division alone manages enough contracts to be listed eighth if it were an independent agency. It also represents athletes in hockey, basketball, baseball, and golf.

Excel Sports Management is the leading agency for professional basketball players, with more than sixty NBA clients. It also represents baseball players and golfers.

Boras Corp employs the top sports agents for baseball. Founder Scott Boras is the most successful agent in history.

Wasserman Media Group is perhaps the most diversified agency in the top five. Its agents represent athletes in football, baseball, basketball, soccer, and golf.

Octagon's clients include players in the NFL, MLB, NBA, and NHL.

THE DOWNSIDE

A sports agent's career does have a downside, though. Income is irregular, and he or she gets paid only when clients get paid. Depending on when sports seasons fall, agents get big windfalls of cash followed by months when no money at all comes in.

For example, NFL agents earn commissions from September through January, so they have no income from February through August. However, they may get money in March if a client signs with a team as a free agent. If the agents represent draft picks, they may see a percentage in May, June, and/or July. At best, that still leaves February, April, and August without payment no matter what. So agents must be good at managing their own money.

Also, agents invest time and money in their clients, providing transportation, housing, meals, and training to the tune of thousands of dollars—as well as paying their own expenses. And success is never guaranteed. If no team signs the athlete, the agent's money and time are lost. Even if the player later signs as a free agent, the agent's commission on the signing bonus seldom equals the outgoing costs.

Although the frenzy of the career is often fun, it's also highly stressful. Another negative factor is the difficulty in finding a balance between work and personal life, especially if the agent has a family. With the necessary extensive travel involved, agents are away from home a lot. Leisure vacations may not be possible at all. Often, depending on the sport, as soon as a season ends, agents hit the road in search of new prospects.

Finally, the business is so competitive that it has been described as cutthroat. Some agents have taken ruthless—and even illegal—measures to sign clients or steal them from other agents. It's easy to understand why. According to ESPN.com, the NFL certified one thousand agents in 2017. However, the top one hundred agents represented 90 percent of the players. The other nine hundred agents were continuously on the hunt for clients.

WHO WAS FIRST?

Credit as the first sports agent in history goes to Charles C. Pyle, who managed a theater in Champagne, Illinois. The city is home to the University of Illinois. Nicknamed "Cash and Carry" Pyle, he was a showman and a natural promoter who realized that professional sports could mean big business opportunities. He became an agent for Harold Edward "Red" Grange, an outstanding halfback for the Fighting Illini who became known as "the Galloping Ghost."

Grange had caused quite a stir in the football world in 1924 when the University of Michigan came to town on a warm Saturday afternoon. The Michigan Wolverines had tied Illinois for the Big Ten championship the year before. Michigan had gone on to win the national championship. Illinois fans were up for a rematch. The highly anticipated game drew sixty-five thousand fans to New Memorial

C. C. "Cash and Carry" Pyle, the first sports agent, promoted the Los Angeles to New York City footrace that became known as the Bunion Derby starting on March 4, 1928.

Stadium, dedicated to students and alumni who served in World War I.

Grange, then a junior running back, returned the kickoff for a 95-yard touchdown. He scored three more times in the first twelve minutes of the game and added a fifth touchdown in the third quarter, thrilling fans and soaring to wide acclaim and national prominence.

Grange hired Pyle to negotiate a deal with the Chicago Bears of what would become the National Football League. The day after Grange's last college football game, he signed the contract. At the time, most professional football players earned just $100 per game. Grange would get $3,000 per game for nineteen games in a barnstorming tour. He also got a share of gate receipts. The deal earned him a cool $100,000. The tour drew huge crowds and helped gain acceptance for professional football as a national sport.

Pyle continued to represent Grange throughout his playing career. The agent also arranged endorsement deals that included a $10,000 royalty plus a percentage of all sales for "approving" a candy bar. Grange also signed a trademark for a line of sporting goods that earned him another $3,500 up front plus a percentage of sales. He got still another $500 simply for being photographed with an outboard motor.

Pyle wasn't through. He lined up roles in two silent movies for the football star: *One Minute to Play* in 1926 and *A Racing Romeo* in 1927. After retiring from football, Grange became a sports announcer for Chicago Bears games as well as for college games, including the Sugar Bowl. Grange has been credited with attracting a huge audience to professional football. And Pyle set the stage for future sports agents in all professional sports.

Chapter 2 STARTING NOW

If you'd like a career as a sports agent, you can start preparing for it even before you graduate from high school. Take stock of your own personal traits. Are you passionate about sports? Do you have charisma? Charisma is a hard-to-define quality of charm, enthusiasm, and personal magnetism that draws others to you. Are you willing to take risks? Can you work on your own without direction from others?

Sports agents deal with athletes, athletes' parents, team managers, coaches, owners, executives, and others in both formal settings, like corporate offices, and casual settings, like parties. The agent's job is easier if he or she is friendly and likable and able to form relationships with many people in different roles. A confident, assertive personality is a must. So is a high sense of integrity. Integrity means more than simple honesty; it also includes strong moral principles.

Agents often take chances on promising athletes who may not succeed in the professional game. Waiting for a client to warrant a top salary with no guarantee of

Building strong relationships with athletes, parents, and coaches is essential for a sports agent like Andrei Mitkov (*right*) who represents Russian Olympic swimmer Yulia Efimova shown with her father/coach.

a payoff requires patience. And, whether agents work for themselves or for a large agency, they must find and sign their own clients. They need discipline and motivation to get the job done. They also need a strong work ethic to help them work the necessary long hours. And they need to be able to multitask—taking care of many clients and their wide variety of needs at the same time.

SKILL SET

To best serve their clients, sports agents need to know a lot about a lot of things. Money-management and financial skills are important. Personal finance principles help agents manage their own irregular income. They also help agents advise clients about budgeting and investing their money.

Business-management skills help agents understand the business side of professional sports. Agents especially need to understand the field of accounting. Accounting is a systematic way to keep track of financial records of a person or business. The process identifies, measures, summarizes, and interprets such information as profit, loss, assets, and liabilities.

An asset in normal conversation can mean anything positive, as in "his running ability is his best asset." However, in accounting an asset is something of value that can be measured in dollars and that can benefit the owner in the future.

Some injuries sideline athletes. Others end careers. Sports agents must know the difference and recommend sports medicine specialists to help clients return to their sports whenever possible.

Examples include cash, stocks and bonds, inventory, land, buildings, and equipment.

A liability is a person's or company's financial obligations owed to another person or company. A loan to buy business equipment is an example of a liability. The total value of assets minus the amount of liabilities is known as net worth. Some of the information accountants assemble is used for financial analysis. Some must be reported to such tax collection entities as state and local treasuries and the federal Internal Revenue Service.

Agents must also understand risk assessment and risk management. Risk assessment identifies potential future events that could pose danger to a person or business, including measuring the likelihood and severity of those events. The assessment may forecast estimated financial loss or simply review threats. Risk management is the process of taking measures to avoid risks or reduce their negative effects.

Many high school business classes teach these skills. The Shawnee Mission School District in Kansas, for example, offers classes in accounting, business law, business management, entrepreneurship, financial literacy, international business, marketing, and personal finance. This curriculum gives students a foundation in the business skills sports agents need. Many schools have in-house stores or other businesses that give students who run and manage them a way to apply the principles learned.

In schools that have business academies, students may have classes in financial and risk assessment and management as well. In addition to the standard math classes in algebra, geometry, and calculus, high school classes in statistics, consumer math, and consumer finance may be offered.

SPEAK EASY

Sports agents need strong communication skills, both oral and written. They must accurately describe their clients' values to professional teams when seeking roster positions or salary increases. Agents need to talk to business owners and charity leaders when arranging endorsements and personal appearances. They also need to understand and be able to modify contract terms. Even such casual communications as email and texting must be professional and easy for recipients to understand.

Good communication forms the basis for building the relationships so crucial to an agent's career. Relationships result from understanding the other person's ideas and emotions. Careful listening helps determine what those are. The agent can then present proposals in terms that are important to the other party.

High school classes in language arts cover composition and technical writing skills aimed at effective writing for different situations and audiences. Students also learn to read for understanding and information

WORKING WELL WITH OTHERS

Strong relationships with athletes, team personnel, and others are critical to a sports agent's career. A good way to build them is through communications skills that make people feel comfortable with you and open to your ideas. Here are some tips for creating a foundation for long-term success:

- *Find common ground. What do you have in common with the other person? For starters, you're both interested in the same sport. What else? Are you from the same state? Did you go to the same college? Do you both collect baseball cards or lapel pins from places you visit?*
- *Use positive phrasing. Instead of saying, "Don't do that," say "Avoid doing that." Avoiding the negative makes communication more pleasant.*
- *Look for ways to compliment the other person. Avoid spewing pure flattery. Be sure the compliment is sincere and warranted.*
- *Remember the person's name. Nothing sounds so beautiful to someone as his or her own name. Include names in greetings and other communication.*
- *Mirror the other person. Without being obvious use the same body language as the other person. For example, if he or she taps a fist on the table to emphasize a point, wait a short while and imitate the movement while making a point of your own.*

by reading a variety of texts. Speech classes teach skills for different purposes and occasions. Speech classes also help students overcome the stage fright that many suffer from at first. High school activities that help develop speech and writing skills include working on the school newspaper or yearbook and competitive speech and drama.

Agents must be persuasive to convince executives, coaches, and managers that a certain player is just who their team needs. Like building relationships, effective persuasion starts with active listening and a focus on the other person's needs. With that in mind, agents list a player's traits and skills in terms of how they will benefit the person they're trying to persuade. They must ensure that their claims can be verified.

Good persuasion skills include research of sports teams' strengths and weaknesses, as well as abilities of other athletes their clients are competing with for a given position. Persuasion involves persistence. Agents sometimes must keep asking for what they want and continuously remind teams of their clients' value.

High school classes and competitive teams in debate and forensics provide opportunities to learn and practice persuading others. Some schools offer classes in argumentation and discussion, as well as legal communication and mock trials.

High school classes in speech and composition help future sports agents gain skills they need to communicate and build relationships with a variety of professional sports personnel.

ON THE FIELD AND IN THE STANDS

Sports agents must be avid sports fans with almost fanatic interest in the sport(s) they represent. Some agents specialize in one sport. However, they should know a lot about all professional sports. They never know when they'll get a chance to sign a player in a different sport. Keeping up with trends in all sports can translate to more clients and, thus, higher earnings.

In high school, get involved in sports in any way you can. If you're an athlete, try out for your school sports teams. Look for a summer job teaching at sports clinics or camps. If you are not an athlete, you can volunteer as a team manager on the bench or spirit leader in the stands. Form relationships with players and coaches as you develop your communications and networking skills.

Or, work as a caddy or as a batboy or batgirl. One Los Angeles–based agent got his start as a caddy on a local golf course. He learned the game and made friends and valuable connections with golfers. That networking led to forming a client base for his sports agency.

Batboys and batgirls pick up Major League Baseball players' bats during games. They also clean cleats and batting helmets and "mud" the baseballs before a game. They rub new baseballs with Lena Blackburne Original Baseball Rubbing Mud to make them easier to grip. The mud comes from the New Jersey shore of the Delaware River. It's been used in Major League Baseball since 1938 and was first used by the Philadelphia Athletics. To qualify for the job of batboy/girl, applicants must be at least fourteen years old and physically fit. To apply, contact a team in the off-season.

Getting a job as a batboy/girl for a Major League Baseball team is a good way to meet athletes, managers, and team administrators while you're still in high school.

POPULAR CULTURE

In addition, follow college and professional sports—even ones beyond the big spectator sports of baseball, basketball, football, hockey, and soccer. Golfers, figure skaters, and tennis stars need agents, too. Watch televised sports to learn to recognize talented athletes in college and professional leagues. Visit sports websites. And read newspaper sports pages and sports magazines online or in hard copy to keep up with current trends in different sports. Pay special attention during draft season and the postseason, which mean more than the regular season to many sports agents and others in the industry.

Two sports magazines for tweens and teens are *Sports Illustrated Kids* and *Junior Baseball. Sports Illustrated Kids* has an iPad version available through iTunes. *Junior Baseball* has an online version. Sports magazines for adults include *International Figure Skating*, *Sports Illustrated*, *Tennis Magazine*, and *USA Today Sports Weekly.*

A classic feature film about a sports agent was released in 1996. *Jerry Maguire* stars Tom Cruise as the lead character. Maguire loses all of his clients except for one egomaniac football player. The movie has been criticized for inaccurate portrayal of the business of sports agency. However, it does illustrate the hectic, cutthroat nature of the job. Cuba Gooding Jr. won an Academy Award for the role of the football player. He uttered the memorable and oft-repeated line "Show me the money!"

Moneyball is an "inside baseball" film based on a true story and released in 2011 with an MPPA PG-13 rating. Actor Brad Pitt plays Billy Beane, general manager of the Oakland A's, who rebuilds his team with a limited budget. He uses a selection system created by a Yale-educated economist that defies conventional wisdom. Instead of using traditional statistics like batting averages and runs batted in, the economist looks for one player quality: he gets on base.

Two more movies that involve the business side of professional sports are *Draft Day* and *Million Dollar*

ART IMITATES LIFE

The role of Jerry Maguire in the movie of the same name was modeled after real-life sports agent Drew Rosenhaus, who made a cameo appearance in the film. With his brother, the agent founded Rosenhaus Sports Representation in Miami, Florida, at the age of twenty-two. Rosenhaus, also known as "the Shark," has a reputation as a relentless agent who stops at nothing to get his clients the best deals. In 2016, Forbes *reported that he earned an estimated $25.2 million in commissions on contracts for sixty-five NFL players worth a total of $839.6 million. According to his agency's website, he has negotiated more than $2 billion in NFL contracts over the course of his career.*

Rosenhaus graduated from the University of Miami and Duke University School of Law. His most valuable clients have included:

- *Antonio Brown, Pittsburg Steelers wide receiver and punt returner*
- *Joe Haden, Cleveland Browns cornerback*
- *Rob "Gronk" Gronkowski, New England Patriots tight end*
- *NaVorro Bowman, San Francisco 49ers linebacker*
- *Sam Shields, free agent cornerback formerly with the Green Bay Packers*
- *Orlando Franklin, Los Angeles Chargers guard*
- *Brian Cushing, Houston Texans inside linebacker*

Billy Beane was the general manager of the Oakland Athletics who fielded a competitive team on a tight budget by signing undervalued baseball players—a feat portrayed in the motion picture *Moneyball*.

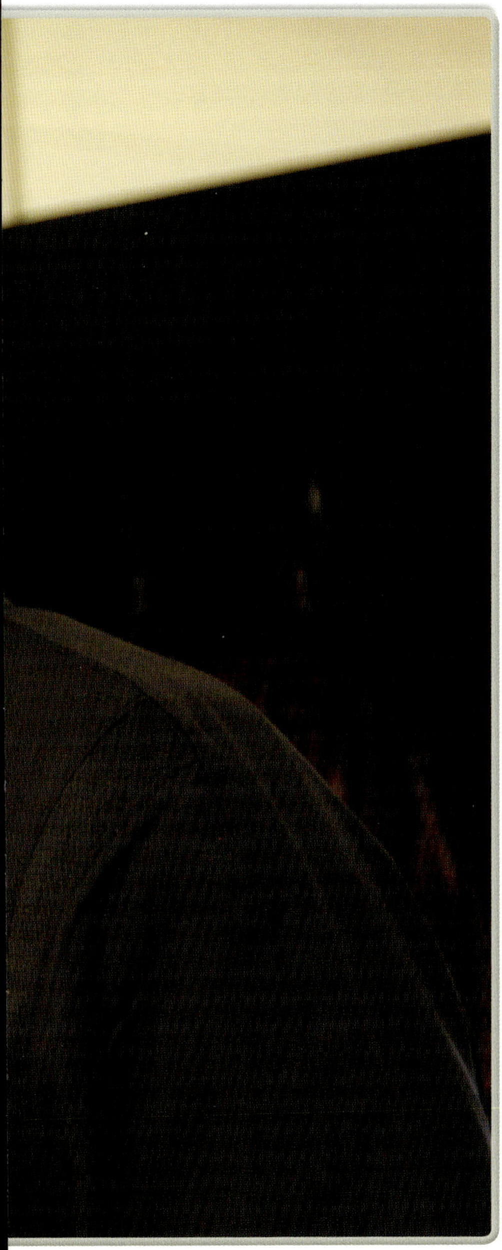

Arm, both 2014 releases. *Draft Day* (MPPA PG-13) stars Kevin Costner as the Cleveland Browns football team's general manager, who has to decide how to use the team's number one draft pick. *Million Dollar Arm* (MPPA PG), based on a true story, stars Jon Hamm as sports agent JB Bernstein who discovers two cricket players from India. The agent tries to get them baseball tryouts, hoping one or both of them will become the next Major League Baseball pitching sensation.

Chapter 3 BE PREPARED

How can you learn what you need to know to become a sports agent? The most common answer is a formal postsecondary education. In some sports a college degree is not an official requirement, but most sports agents have at least a bachelor's degree. Many have master's degrees or complete law school. In fact, the NFL Players Association requires football agents to have a master's degree or law degree. In any sport, the career is highly competitive. A college degree increases your chances of getting a job as an agent.

Some programs, primarily those offered online, offer sports agent courses that can be completed in a matter of weeks. These may be a good way to add to what you know about the career after you have earned a bachelor's degree. They cover such specific topics as client recruitment, contract negotiation, legal and financial issues, marketing and endorsements, post-career counseling, ethics, and compliance with laws, rules, and regulations of universities, professional leagues, states, and the federal government.

In the competitive world of sports agents, a bachelor's, master's, or law degree is essential. Many colleges and universities offer majors in sport management, business administration, or related fields.

These types of programs enhance knowledge, but they are not valid substitutes for college degrees. Instead, look for college or university degree programs that cover subjects that pertain to sports agency. Even if you built a foundation of these with high school classes, now's the time to study them in depth.

OFF TO COLLEGE

At the bachelor's degree level, major in sports management, sports administration, marketing, business administration, or accounting. Focus on courses in public relations, communications, marketing, math and statistics, psychology, negotiation, financial planning, investments, and tax, sports, and contract law. Some sports management degrees include the study of fitness and are offered in kinesiology or exercise science departments. According to the American Kinesiology Association, kinesiology is the academic discipline that involves the "study of physical activity and its impact on health, society, and quality of life." In short, it's the scientific study of the anatomy and mechanics of human movement.

The more you know, the better sports agent you'll be. Sports agents need broad knowledge of financial planning, contract law, negotiating, marketing, and many aspects of athletics.

For a master's degree, try to supplement your knowledge. For instance, if you earned a bachelor's degree in sports management, work toward a master's in business administration, also known as an MBA. Or, major in business at the bachelor's level and get a master's in sports management.

Agents need knowledge of tax law, contract law, business law, and other legal issues. That's why many agents are tax attorneys or have advanced degrees in sports law or contract law. Along with negotiating contracts, agents often make or recommend financial decisions for their clients. Agents must also know how to protect their clients from the threat of lawsuits. Without a law degree, an agent can offer services but should hire a lawyer to prepare legal documents and negotiate and/or review contracts.

Another way to prepare for a career as a sports agent is to become a certified public accountant (CPA). Requirements vary by state. They include education, examination, and experience. Education must include a bachelor's degree, a passing grade on the nationwide CPA exam, and one or two years' experience working with a CPA. If you major in accounting, join the American Institute of CPAs as a student affiliate member. Benefits include scholarship opportunities, competitions, discounts on conferences, access to industry publications, and discounts on products and services.

While in college find a way to make a connection to the sports world. You'll be able to relate to athletes if you have a background as a player or if you have extensive knowledge about sports or a particular sport. Follow trends in player salaries and benefits through media reports. Become familiar with the rules of the sports leagues you're interested in. Pay special attention to any changes in league collective-bargaining agreements.

NETWORKING FOR COLLEGIANS

College students studying sports management or related subjects can start connecting with the sports world in their own school or department through activities with college athletics. Some networking ideas include:

- *Getting to know athletes on your school's teams*
- *Getting to know the professors and staff*
- *Joining clubs or organizations in your field of study*
- *Offering to conduct research for a faculty member for free*
- *Volunteering as a student aide in the department office*
- *Volunteering to escort guest speakers on campus*
- *Getting good grades and asking to be considered for honorary societies*

ON-THE-JOB TRAINING

With plenty of "book learning" under your belt, the next thing you need is the ability to identify and cultivate talent. That comes with experience. It sounds like a chicken and egg situation. You can't get a job as a sports agent without experience. But you can't get experience without a job.

Internships fill that role. An internship is a temporary paid or unpaid job for the purpose of gaining practical work experience. The idea for internship was derived from apprenticeships in medieval times. Craftsmen taught

An internship with a sports agency offers on-the-job training, one of the best ways to start a career in professional sports management.

their trades to younger individuals. The apprentices "paid" for the training by working for the teachers for a specified period. Today's internships do not require the interns to make a commitment to the business that offers the program. And the employers are not expected to hire the interns—although many companies do offer positions to interns who do a good job.

FIND A SPOT

Finding a sports-management internship involves some research. Several websites offer tips. One is the site for the Black Sports Agents Association. Its Student Internship Program selects top students who have an interest in sports for internships in public relations, marketing, law, advertising, management, agency/representation, financial services, and promotions.

At ESPN.com, college students currently enrolled in a degree program can apply for fall, spring, or summer paid internships offered in Bristol, Connecticut; New York, New York; Austin, Texas; Charlotte, North Carolina; or Los Angeles, California. Interns work forty hours per week for ten weeks. This site is part of the Disney Professional Internship Program.

Internships.com is a free website that lists internships in many fields, including sports management. You can enter your career goal, location, and whether you'll take paid or unpaid positions. The website also has tips about applying and preparing for interviews.

LookSharp.com is a free website where students can search for sports internships. The site also features an active forum, an intern blog, and sample cover letters and résumés.

The Sports Agent Blog lists internships with sports agencies and firms specializing in sports law. It also features interviews with active sports agents and news articles about the world of professional sports.

The Sports Job Board is a good place to look for internships in professional sports. It also lists openings for "real" jobs in sports.

At Sports Management Worldwide, students who apply for internships must first complete one of the company's sports career training courses. Internships are offered in Portland, Oregon, and Gloucester, England. The unpaid internships cover such areas as sports marketing, sports agency, scouting reports, player contracts, and more. They require twenty hours per week for at least three months.

WorkInSports.com features a database of sports internships as well as jobs. Searching the database is free, but to apply for any of the internships requires a paid subscription.

In addition, colleges and universities often have connections to internship programs or can arrange an

For sports agents, learning continues after college. To maintain their credentials, agents must attend annual seminars and pass written tests administered by professional players associations.

internship for their students. Ask a professor or visit your department head's office.

You can also apply directly to a sports agent or sports agency. Some agency websites that list internship opportunities include Creative Artists Agency, IMG, Octagon, Pro Stars Sports Agency, and Wasserman.

BECOMING CERTIFIED

If you plan to represent athletes in professional baseball, basketball, football, or hockey, you must be certified by the sports players association. Certification requirements include a background check and your agreement to follow ethical standards.

You'll need to pass the league's sports agent exam. There's an examination fee, as well as dues to be paid to the league. In addition to certification requirements by players associations, some states, including Georgia, New York, and Florida, require licensure or registration of agents who represent athletes.

Players associations for each sport determine the qualifications and requirements for agents. The NFL, for example, requires a master's degree or law degree from an accredited college or university. It has a nonrefundable application fee, according to the NFL Players Association (NFLPA) website. Application dates are posted, and no early or late entries are accepted. Those whose applications are approved must attend a two-day seminar and pass a written test.

The test covers the collective bargaining agreement, salary cap, player benefits, players association regulations about contract advisers, policies about substance abuse and performance-enhancing substances, and other issues. Prospective agents may not recruit or represent athletes until they have passed the exam, paid a fee, and purchased professional liability insurance.

Once certified, agents must continue to maintain certification by paying an annual fee and attending an NFLPA annual seminar. Certified agents must also negotiate at least one player contract every three years. Financial planners who work for NFL players do not need certification, but there is a voluntary program that defines standards for handling athletes' finances.

In baseball, the Major League Baseball Players Association (MLBPA) requires a previously uncertified agent to agree to MLBPA regulations for player agents. You must pay an application fee, according to the MLBPA website, and applicants must pass a written exam. Before being certified, applicants must be designated as a major league player's agent, recruiter, client maintenance service provider, or expert agent adviser.

The National Basketball Association Players Association (NBPA) requires agents to have a degree from an accredited four-year college or university. Relevant negotiating experience may be considered in lieu of any year(s) of college coursework. According to the NBPA website, applications must be accompanied by a nonrefundable fee and agent dues. The dues will be refunded if the application is rejected or the applicant fails the required written examination. Application dates are posted, and no applications will be accepted outside the time period.

Those whose applications are approved may (but are not required to) attend a review session before taking the required fifty-question multiple-choice examination. The test covers the NBA Collective Bargaining Agreement, the NBPA regulations for player agents, and

Sports agents for professional soccer are called intermediaries. The Fédération Internationale de Football Association (FIFA) requires intermediaries to have "good character and reputation." Each country determines its own requirements.

other topics. Applicants can use prepared notes during the three-hour open book test.

To maintain certification, agents must continue to comply with regulations, pay an annual fee, attend an annual NBPA agent seminar, and negotiate at least one player contract every five years. They must also pay annual dues according to the number of players they represented in the previous season. According to the NBPA website, agents with zero to nine players pay a base rate of dues. Agents with ten to nineteen clients pay twice the base rate. And agents with twenty or more clients pay three times the base rate.

To be certified as an agent for athletes in the National Hockey League Players' Association (NHLPA), an applicant must complete a mandatory agent certification program. The program covers standards of professional conduct and education that certified agents must maintain. Applicants submit a detailed questionnaire concerning their educational and professional background. Information about fees and other issues is sent to those whose applications are approved.

As of 2017, the Major League Soccer Players Union had no agent regulations, certification process, or exam. Until 2001, the Fédération Internationale de Football Association (FIFA), the international governing body for soccer, licensed agents for professional players. Since then, associations from an applicant's home country have determined requirements and issued licenses.

In 2015, FIFA replaced the FIFA Players' Agents Regulations with the new Regulations on Working with Intermediaries, thus replacing the term "agent" with "intermediary." To become an intermediary, an applicant registers by signing an agreement to follow the rules and paying a registration fee. The fee differs in every country. Applicants must also pass the "Test of Good Character and Reputation for Intermediaries." Anyone who has been convicted of financial or violent crimes will be rejected. Intermediaries who will work with minors need special authorization from their country's governing body.

Once registered, an intermediary needs a representation contract with a player or club. The contract must include the names of the parties, nature of legal relationship, scope of services, duration, payment terms, date of completion, termination provisions, and signatures of both parties. There are no limits on how long the contract can stay in effect.

Chapter 4 GET A JOB

Now you're ready to do what all parents dream their college kids will do: seek gainful employment. The best way to start your career is by signing on with an established sports agency where you can get more industry experience and meet clients and prospective clients.

At first you might specialize in just one of the services the agency offers. If so, you'll gain expertise in career management, contract negotiations, draft preparation, marketing and endorsements, media relations, or other areas of the business. Look for an agency with a good reputation and lots of clients, preferably in a variety of sports. Check online job boards and individual agencies' websites for listings of current openings.

Internet searches of online job boards and sports agency websites are good ways to find job openings in the professional sports industry.

LOOKIN' GOOD ON PAPER

Start by preparing a résumé. A résumé is a document that lists your education, work experience, and activities. Its purpose is to get an interview. It's your first chance to convince employers that you're right for the job. It must be true and accurate and show you in the best possible light.

Visit an agency's website and read its media releases. Tailor a new résumé for each position you apply for, emphasizing your strengths in terms of the opening. A good résumé should stress accomplishments rather than responsibilities. Whenever possible, use specific numbers to quantify your results. Instead of saying, "Responsible for group sales in the university's athletic ticket office," say something like, "Increased group sales in the university's athletic ticket office by 15 percent over the previous year."

A résumé should look good. Use "normal" fonts and plenty of white space. Avoid fancy script or a crowded appearance on the page. Use 10-point or 12-point Times New Roman or Arial. Be sure grammar and spelling are correct. And use the same style throughout the document. For instance, if you use bullet points in one section, don't switch to dashes in another. The same goes for using bold, italics, or underlining.

Organize the document according to what you have to offer. If you're in college or you're a recent graduate without significant sports-related experience, list education first. List your major and minor (if any), your grade point average (GPA), and related courses outside the major. For example, if you majored in sports management, list additional business courses you completed. If you're an athlete or have related work experience, move education to the end of the document.

Work experience should be listed with the most recent jobs first, especially any related to sports, sales, or

A résumé for a job in a sports agency should emphasize the applicant's experience and passion for sports as a player, volunteer, or employee in some aspect of athletics.

promotions. Include a section for college activities and awards. List sports-related ones first. If you participated in sports or sports activities in high school, put them down, too. You want to project your passion for sports every way

TALK TO ME

Try to find a sports agent willing to talk to you in an information interview. An information interview is a conversation with a professional to learn about the field and local job market. Ask for an appointment for fifteen or twenty minutes. Remember that sports agents are always busy, so if you get an appointment, respect your time limit.

Make a list of questions to ask. Some typical questions include:

- *How did you become sports agent?*
- *What do you like best and least about the job?*
- *What tips do you have for someone starting out?*
- *Do you know of any jobs right now?*

Afterward, thank the agent. Leave your name and contact information in case he or she later learns of a job opening you might be a good fit for. Send a thank-you email or handwritten thank-you note. Add the agent to your growing list of contacts in the business of professional sports. From time to time, drop the agent a note or email to stay in touch. When you land a job, let him or her know where you are working and again give thanks for the help.

you can. Also list any additional skills. For instance, being bilingual can be a real asset in recruiting foreign athletes. Being a club officer shows leadership.

Put contact information on top. Create a separate email address for the purpose of job hunting—perhaps just your name or initials. Avoid quirky user names that look unprofessional. Also, review your social media presence and publicly available information to be sure it reflects a professional attitude and lifestyle. Many employers do basic searches of social media websites to identify potential concerns about a candidate, so it's a good idea to review your own publicly available information.

LET'S MEET

After you apply for a sports agent job, the next step is a job interview. A job interview is a conversation between an employer and a potential employee. The employer's goal is to find a new employee. Your goal is to get a job. When you make an appointment, ask for the name of the person you will talk to.

Immediately start preparing for the interview. Find out everything you can about the employer and the person(s) who will interview you. Look for them on Facebook, LinkedIn, Google+, and other social media. Search the company website for stated goals, leaders, and recent

Employers use job interviews to determine how well an applicant will fit into the corporate culture. Applicants evaluate how the opening fits their career goals.

news releases. Also search for newspaper and magazine articles about the company and its leadership.

Practice for your interview with parents or friends. Look online or in books for typical job interview questions. Think about possible answers, but don't try to memorize them. You'll want to appear spontaneous and genuine, not scripted. Your interviewer wants to get a sense of what you're like and how you will fit into the agency. Be prepared to discuss items on your résumé. Keep in mind that you're likely to be asked about other topics, too.

THE DAY OF THE INTERVIEW

Arrive for the interview between five and ten minutes early. Turn off your mobile phone before entering the office. If there is a receptionist, be friendly and professional. Some employers ask the receptionist how applicants act in the waiting area.

When you meet your interviewer, repeat his or her name as you make eye contact. Firmly shake hands. Appear confident, but not cocky. Wait to be invited to sit. Look for anything personal in the office that you can relate to. Try to create a personal connection. Carefully listen to the interviewer's questions. Make eye contact and smile before you answer.

Ask your own questions. Keep in mind that the more you let the interviewer talk, the more he or she will like you! Ask about the agency and specific clients based on your research to show that you took the time to be informed. Ask such questions as: What duties will I perform at first? What opportunities will there be for me to learn more and gain more experience? Must I recruit my own clients?

Avoid questions about benefits or vacations. Instead, focus on what you can contribute. Ask if there will be more interviews (often there will be more than one). Ask when they expect to make a decision. Most important: ask for the job. It's unlikely that you'll be

FIND A MENTOR

Finding a mentor in the sports business boosts the chances for a successful career. Rick Curran was a successful college ice hockey player at Merrimack College and later became international hockey coordinator for Hockey Canada. Later still he became business manager for Team Canada.

Before becoming an agent, he first worked at a sports-management company as an assistant to an agent named Bill Watters in Toronto, Canada. Curran first met Watters eleven years earlier when Curran was an instructor at the Bobby Orr Hockey Camp and Watters was camp director. The ten summers Curran worked there gave him the opportunity to meet people in the sport.

"What I did, and what I would recommend to anyone who wants to get into this business, is that I made myself absolutely indispensable," Curran said on the College Foundation of North Carolina website. "In other words, (Watters) couldn't go anywhere without me. I made it my business to know all the junior players, pro players. If (Watters) needed to know something, I was the answer man."

Acting as Watters's assistant gave Curran the experience he needed to become an agent himself. Now a well-known hockey agent with the Orr Hockey Group, Curran began as a sports agent in 1978. He earned millions in 2016, according to Forbes.

He negotiated contracts worth over $400 million for such National Hockey League clients as:

- Jordan Staal and Jeff Skinner, Carolina Hurricanes
- Taylor Hall, New Jersey Devils
- Jeff Carter, Los Angeles Kings
- Tomáš Plekanec, Montreal Canadiens
- Patrick Sharp and Jason Spezza, Dallas Stars

hired on the spot. But it doesn't hurt to ask. When the interviewer stands, it's time to leave. At the end of the interview, smile, and shake hands again. Use the interviewer's name.

After the interview send an email or handwritten thank-you note and again express interest in the job. You may or may not be contacted if you don't get the job. So, check back in a few days or a week via phone or email. Ask about the status of the opening. If the job has been filled, thank the interviewer. Ask to be considered for future openings. Apply elsewhere.

If you want to get a job with a sports agency but can't find one, look for something in the field of professional sports. Adding work experience will give you opportunities to learn about the business and strengthen your résumé for future work as a sports agent.

ON YOUR OWN

Instead of working in an agency, some sports agents work as freelancers or start their own businesses. A freelance worker works for another business independently on a self-employed basis, filling in for regular staff. To start you'll need significant funding. You'll pay your own expenses, as well as travel, lodging, and training expenses for clients—

Independent sports agents pay their own travel and other expenses with no guarantee their efforts will pay off in signing clients and getting them professional sports contracts.

all with no guarantee of future income. Establishing yourself can take many years and many thousands of dollars.

Be sure to buy agent insurance or a surety bond. A surety bond is a three-party contract between an agent, an athlete, and the surety company. The bond protects clients from any illegal or unethical actions on the agent's part. The surety company covers any resulting losses. You'll have to maintain your certifications and pay league fees to stay active.

Rely on all of your strengths. Decide which services to offer clients and set your rates. In the beginning keep your prices low. You can raise them

Communication is the key to a successful sports agent career. Agents need the most up-to-date computers and mobile devices, including the ability to use video conferencing on the go.

later. Finally, decide which sport or sports to specialize in. Become an expert on the rules and players in that sport. For tools of the trade, you'll want top-of-the-line smartphones, computers, and other communications devices, including video-conferencing ability. You'll also need a reliable calculator and comfortable shoes that support days with long hours on your feet.

Most of all, though, you'll need clients.

BREAKING IN

Don't expect to sign a top pro athlete as your first client. Instead, start small. Look for graduating college players or minor league players just starting out in the professional game. Join sports organizations. Go to parties. Attend showcases and college scouting events. And never stop networking. Many sports agents build their client list from referrals from others in the industry.

You'll likely have to make some cold calls. A cold call is an unsolicited contact in an effort to sell something—in this case, your services. Show confidence and enthusiasm. Work to establish and keep a good reputation.

To convince a prospect of your ability, create a business plan for him or her. A business plan is a package that includes a mission statement for the athlete, as well as potential marketing ideas, and a plan for training the athlete in preparation for showcases, showcase tournaments, and drafts. A good business plan will be concise and easy to understand.

At first, most of your efforts will be focused on adding new clients. (New clients will crop up in a variety of ways, so always have your mind open to networking.) But as you grow, be sure to strike a balance between servicing current clients and adding new ones.

Chapter 5
SEE YOU IN COURT

If you're a sports agent and you're not a lawyer, you may need to hire one. Legal issues are at the heart of athlete representation. Sports agents must understand tax law, labor law, financial regulations, and more at the federal, state, and local levels. Other legal areas include salary caps and intellectual property rights. And, agents are responsible for seeing that their employees follow all laws, rules, regulations, and guidelines that apply to their business.

Agents need full understanding of contracts between players and owners. For example, the Major League Baseball Players Agreement covers such topics as when a player can become a free agent, negotiating rules that apply before the free-agent period, and how free agents and newly drafted players can be signed. Likewise, recruiting rules for each sport vary but must be followed. For example, high schools students can sign with agents for Major League Baseball and the National Hockey League.

Sports agents must know and follow rules for recruiting athletes to avoid jeopardizing players' eligibility for National Collegiate Athletic Association competition.

However, a college football player loses eligibility for the National Collegiate Athletic Association (NCAA) games if he signs before the last game of his senior year.

Agents are also likely to be called on if a client gets arrested for illegal gambling, assault and battery at a late-night fight, or other crime. If a player gets hit with a civil lawsuit, he or she is likely to call the agent first. A civil lawsuit is a court case between two or more individuals, businesses, government, or other entities. Typically, the person who sues seeks to recover money,

IT'S A CRIME

In 1985, Norby Walters, a longtime agent for entertainers in show business, branched out and added a sports agency to his business. As noted in Playing for Keeps by Chris Mortensen, the agent, along with Lloyd Bloom, offered $800,000 to around fifty athletes as part of an agreement to represent them when they turned pro.

The Federal Bureau of Investigation (FBI) got wind of the activities and launched a seventeen-month-long investigation that tied the men to organized crime. A federal grand jury indicted Walters and Bloom on eight counts of conspiracy to commit extortion, racketeering, and mail fraud. The indictment also alleged that they threatened players who took the money but failed to sign contracts. (One athlete claimed that Bloom told him, "We can get someone from Vegas to come down and see that [you] don't play football again.") The agents faced a total of seventy years in prison, $2 million in fines, and forfeiture of their sports business. The agents were convicted in 1989, but the verdict was overturned on appeal.

not punish or imprison the other party (parties). Some events involve both criminal and civil prosecution in separate cases.

While the athlete may need to hire his or her own lawyers in these situations, the agent must coordinate media inquiries with an eye to minimize damage to the player's image, reputation, or other interests.

WHO, ME?

Agents might need legal advice for their own interests. For example, state regulations in Florida and Texas are so strict that agents who have failed to comply have spent time in jail.

At the very least, agents need in-depth knowledge of two particular laws. The first is a federal law known as the Sports Agent Responsibility and Trust Act (SPARTA). The other is a state law in effect in most states called the Uniform Athlete Agents Act (UAAA).

Professional athletes may need legal advice, but so may sports agents, who must obey state and federal laws designed to protect players.

SPARTA falls under the Federal Trade Commission Act, which protects businesses and individuals from unfair or deceptive acts. SPARTA's purpose is to make improper conduct of athlete agents illegal. It protects student athletes from activities associated with signing a representation contract. The law bans agents from using false or misleading information or promises to sign a client. Agents may not give anything of value (gifts, cash, or loans) to the student athlete or anyone associated with him or her. It requires agents to communicate in writing that any would-be client may lose NCAA eligibility by signing an agency contract.

Violating the law is considered an unfair or deceptive act. SPARTA empowers state attorneys general, as well as colleges and universities, to bring civil lawsuits to recover any damages caused by agents who fail to follow the provisions. Violators can also be prosecuted under the Federal Trade Act. Under the act, punishment for an unfair or deceptive practice can be a several-thousand-dollar fine.

SPARTA defines three duties of sports agents: a duty to be truthful, a duty of disclosure, and a duty to refrain from "buying" an athlete.

PROTECTING STUDENT ATHLETES

Practices of some sports agents can cause significant damage to student athletes' eligibility for NCAA competition, as well as harsh penalties imposed on teams and colleges and universities. The UAAA seeks to protect players and their institutions. UAAA is a state law that has been enacted in more than forty states.

Like SPARTA, UAAA focuses on the relationships among agents, student athletes, and educational institutions. The law protects players and schools by regulating agent practices. Originally put forth in 2000, UAAA was updated in 2015. The new version provides for agent registration across state lines. It also adds new requirements for agency contracts and notification and requires agents to give prospective clients important information they can use to evaluate the agent. It prohibits agents from "illegally luring" college athletes into contracts.

It also expands the definition of "agent" to include financial advisers, business managers, and marketers and bars them from making gifts or donating services that affect athletes' NCAA eligibility. Instead of requiring agents to notify colleges once an athlete who still has NCAA eligibility has signed a contract, the updated version requires agents to tell schools before contacting players, their families, or others close to them. The NCAA supports adoption of the law in every state.

The UAAA includes criminal, civil, and administrative penalties. The law's structure varies by state. States designate which practices are felonies and which are misdemeanors. States are also responsible for enforcement. The UAAA recommends fines for violations, but states

National Football League player D. J. Fluker was included in accusations by Yahoo! Sports of illegal sports agent practices involving him and other University of Alabama athletes.

determine the actual amounts of the fines. The original UAAA recommended fines that can total more than $25,000.

In 2013, Yahoo! Sports reported allegations that University of Alabama offensive tackle D. J. Fluker and four other Southeast Conference athletes received benefits from former University of Alabama football player Luther Davis. The media outlet said Davis acted as a middleman between players and several agents and financial advisers. Yahoo! Sports claimed records existed that totaled tens of thousands of dollars worth of cash, airfare, living expenses, and other benefits. If proven, the actions violated Alabama's sports agent laws.

According to those laws, anyone acting as an agent without being licensed by the Alabama Athlete Agents Commission commits a Class C felony, with penalties up to ten years in prison and thousands of dollars in fines. Initiating contact with a college athlete without being registered is a Class A misdemeanor punishable with up to one year in prison and a large fine. In Alabama, college athletes must first sign a contract that conforms to state law with an agent before they're allowed to accept anything of value from him or her.

The Alabama laws resulted from the discovery that University of Alabama football player Antonio Langham had signed a secret contract with an agent. NCAA sanctions forced the school to forfeit most of its 1993 season.

Yahoo! Sports claimed that Davis acted on behalf of registered agents Andy Simms, Peter Schaffer, and John Phillips. The media outlet reported that Davis was not registered in Alabama. Neither were financial advisers Jason Jernigan, Mike Rowan, and Hodge Brahmbhatt, also named in the report as having ties with Davis. Jernigan declined comment. The rest of the agents and advisers confirmed transferring money to Davis but denied telling Davis to give anything of value to the players or even knowing about it. No record of prosecution in the case was found.

IN COURT

The last thing an agent wants to do is end up in court. However publicity about some high-profile cases may affect how the general public views the business of sports agency—especially in terms of the sometimes cutthroat nature of it. Disputes arise between agents and former employers, between agents and athletes, and between competing agents, among other parties.

For example, in 2015 NFL certified agent Sean Howard filed suit against Octagon Inc., in the San Francisco Division of the US District Court for the Northern District of California. Howard asked the court to void noncompete clauses in his contract with the sports management company, his former employer from 2006 to the day before he filed the lawsuit. Howard also claimed that the company engaged in unfair practices and asked the court to order Octagon to return profits and fees it collected from him.

Howard, a former linebacker at the University of California Los Angeles (UCLA), earned a law degree from the University of Oregon. He served in player personnel management with the San Francisco 49ers and Green Bay Packers before joining Octagon as an agent. At Octagon, he represented—among others—first-round draftees defensive end Lawrence Jackson (Minnesota Vi-

kings), tight end Brandon Pettigrew (Detroit Lions), and quarterback Brandon Weeden (Cleveland Browns). Howard left Octagon and started PRIME Athletes, his own "athlete and sports personality representation/brand and business development company."

However, Howard's contract with Octagon prohibited him from working for Octagon competitors. It also placed a one-year restriction on doing business with anyone that Octagon employees had worked with during the six months before he left. Other constraints included a two-year prohibition on soliciting or providing services to Octagon clients and a one-year ban on hiring any Octagon employees who worked during the last six months before the agent left. Finally, the

In lawsuits settled in 2015 without revealing terms, professional golfer Rory McIlroy sued to nullify his contract with sports agent Conor Ridge because of deceptive practices. Ridge countersued.

contract required Howard to pay percentages of fees received in connection with Octagon clients.

Howard wanted the court to declare the restrictions void because they violated the California Business and Professions Code, which prohibits such employer restrictions. No results of the suit were publicized.

OFF THE LINKS

Also in 2015, a Dublin, Ireland, court announced that Conor Ridge, the lead agent of Horizon Sports Management, settled a lawsuit against world-ranked golfer Rory McIlroy. Although terms were not published, the British press placed the amount of the settlement at close to $20 million USD (more than £13 million GBP).

McIlroy, who had won four major tournaments, ended his association with Ridge in 2013. He claimed he had signed the contract "in circumstances of great informality" and was misled about its contents. He denied seeing a copy before he signed it. Horizon countersued for breach of contract and for millions of dollars in commissions the company said the athlete owed it. Among the deals in question was commission on an endorsement deal with athletic shoe and apparel retailer Nike, Inc. that promised the golfer $100 million over five years.

McIlroy said he terminated his contract with Horizon because he didn't like the rates the agency charged him. The deal called for commissions of 5 percent of pretax prize winnings and 20 percent of endorsements and appearances, according to the *New York Post*. McIlroy claimed fellow golfer Graeme McDowell got a better deal from the same agency.

GRAND THEFT ATHLETE

A lawsuit filed by NFL agent Joby Branion against fellow agent Carmen Wallace of Roc Nation Sports made headlines late in 2016. The case stemmed from accusations that Wallace allegedly slandered him and stole his client, Los Angeles Chargers linebacker Melvin Ingram. Slander is a false spoken statement that harms another person's reputation.

Branion and Wallace had worked together at the Athletes First agency. In 2014, Branion started his own agency, the Vanguard Sports Group. He took many of his clients along, including Denver Broncos linebacker Von Miller. According to the complaint, Branion offered to add Wallace's name to Miller's contract under the condition that Wallace would receive no commission on the player's team contract that Branion had negotiated. The contract earned Miller the most ever for a defensive player in the history of the NFL.

Branion charged that Wallace later contacted the player and asked for half of the commission. The two agents argued but agreed to let the athlete decide how

Sports agent Joby Branion (*left*) gets ready to meet with Von Miller (*seated in light pants*). Branion sued fellow agent Carmen Wallace over a contract dispute involving the NFL player.

much to pay to whom. Branion alleged that Wallace untruthfully accused Branion of violating NFL Players Association regulations and that he risked being sanctioned.

In another part of the complaint Branion claimed Wallace contacted Los Angeles Charger Ingram, trying to get him to leave Branion and sign with Wallace. The player did but later returned to Branion. Still later, Wallace allegedly made a side deal with Ingram and Roc Nation Sports that enticed the player to sign a contract for representation by Roc Nation Sports. Roc Nation was founded in 2013 by Shawn Corey Carter, also known as rapper Jay Z. The case was still pending mid-2017.

Chapter 6
LOOKING DOWN THE ROAD

The future outlook for sports agents is hard to determine. The US Bureau of Labor Statistics groups sports agents with business managers and representatives of actors, artists, and other entertainers. The bureau projects those occupations will grow by 10 percent between 2012 and 2020. That rate is about the same as the average for all occupations. As of the late 2010s, an estimated total of three thousand sports agents represented clients across all professional sports.

The field is extremely competitive because only a limited number of roster spots are available on men's professional baseball, basketball, football, hockey, and soccer teams. More opportunities exist in the women's market. However, women's salaries and winnings offer lower commissions than male athletes produce.

In addition to their male counterparts, female professional athletes like those in the Women's National Basketball Association (WNBA) are potential clients for sports agents.

LADIES AND GENTLEMEN

Kelli Masters, one of the few female sports agents in the business, successfully represents some top NFL players—including first-round draft picks and Super Bowl winners. She grew up in Oklahoma City, Oklahoma, and attended her first football game before she started kindergarten. From that first game, she continued to love the excitement of the sport.

At the University of Oklahoma, Masters studied journalism and political science. She also twirled baton

Attending the University of Oklahoma gave sports agent Kelli Masters a way to further her passion for football. One of the few female agents, she represents several NFL players.

during halftime at every football game. During her senior year, she served an internship at the local CBS affiliate and stayed on as an affiliate producer. That experience taught her about broadcast media and marketing. She went on to law school, never imagining she would become one of the few female certified NFL agents in the male-dominated field of sports agency.

In 1998, she entered the Miss Oklahoma pageant of the Miss America contest. She hoped to win a scholarship to pay for law school. She won! As Miss Oklahoma, she had to take off a year of school to prepare to compete for Miss America. She also had to travel throughout Oklahoma, fulfilling contracted obligations for parades, speaking engagements, and personal appearances. In retrospect, the seven-days-per-week travel that year prepared her for the hectic travel she would need to do as a sports agent.

After law school, Masters got a job at a law firm and went to work. Along with dealing with clients' legal proceedings, she worked with nonprofit organizations. One day in 2003, she heard from Josh Heupel, a former star quarterback for the Sooners. He needed help setting up his #14 Foundation, a charity that holds events to raise money for needy children. Along with doing the legal work to establish the foundation, Masters offered advice on its business plan and marketing. Her work for Heupel led to similar interest from other athletes.

"I started asking questions about their world," she told *Cosmopolitan*, "how they were managed, whether anyone had asked them their goals and dreams, and what they wanted their legacy to be. I kept hearing, 'I wish you had been here from the beginning.'"

"Players were coming out of college, some of them from backgrounds where they never had the opportunities or the money or the platform before. Now, so much obligation and opportunity was being placed in their hands. I found that most players and families were not really getting the guidance they needed."

Their agents negotiated contracts, but they seldom helped the athletes make the most out of their opportunities to make money, help their communities, or build a legacy. That's what Masters wanted to do.

WOMEN WON'T "MAKE IT"

Masters called Kristen Kuliga, one of the first female NFL agents, for advice. Kuliga answered her questions about the industry. However, when Masters called her male counterparts, she got no help at all.

The NFL Players Association certified Masters as an agent in 2005. The same year, she signed her first client, Texas Tech quarterback Cody Hodges. Mutual friends introduced them, and she represented him when he signed with the Tennessee Titans as a free agent. Soon after, she attended her first NFL combine. A well-known male agent approached her and lectured her on why women were "never going to make it in this business."

As she told *Cosmopolitan*, she told the man, "You're going to have to get used to me being around, because I'm going to be successful in this business."

Since then, her client list has grown, but it took five more years before one of her players was a first-round draft pick. In 2010, Gerald McCoy was the third player chosen. In 2017, McCoy was still an active player as a defensive tackle for the Tampa Bay Buccaneers. Even today Masters faces tough competition with male agents who continue to

GIRLS ONLY

Due to her own experiences with sports agents, Jeanne McNulty-King started 2X Inc., a full-service sports agency in 1998. The agency specializes in female athletes, particularly players in the Women's National Basketball Association (WNBA).

McNulty-King had played basketball at the University of Montana. When she graduated, she signed with an agent, who secured a contract for her to play professional ball in Spain. However, when she arrived overseas, her passport and ticket home were confiscated by team officials. She also got a new contract with far less favorable terms than the original one she had signed. Efforts to contact her agent were unsuccessful. In fact, she never heard from him again. She was on her own to get back her passport and ticket and find a way home to the United States.

Four months later, she heard from a new agent. This time she was able to continue her playing career in Sydney, Australia. She had positive experiences, both with her agent and with playing outside the United States. "I feel very fortunate, now, to have experienced both good and bad overseas," McNulty-King says on her agency's website. "It gives me perspective into my players' situations. I can think back and remember what I needed and provide that to my players. I also think it is very important to just be there for the players, providing friendship and support."

Her business philosophy includes a commitment to give her clients the kinds of service and support she needed as a professional athlete herself. Her agency has foreign contacts, and she has successfully placed players as a licensed agent for both the WNBA and the International Basketball Federation (FIBA).

tell recruits not to sign with a woman if they want teams to take them seriously.

Nevertheless, she continues to serve her clients both on and off the field, as well as after their playing days are over. Like her first client, many have started foundations that benefit youth. Some have served needy families in their communities. Others have taken humanitarian trips to such places as Haiti and Uganda. Masters wants not only to help her clients have a profitable playing career, but also to create a legacy and go on to live a successful life.

THE WORKPLACE

A majority of sports agents work for international sports management agencies. Some work on their own or on staff at a law firm. No matter where their offices are, however, most of them do a lot of work in their cars. Sports agents are on the road almost every day. They travel extensively to recruit clients, watch games, meet with sports organizations, and more. And their mobile phones connect them to the sports world twenty-four hours a day, seven days a week, whether they're in a big city or on a beach somewhere.

Earnings range widely. An agent's income depends on the number of clients represented and how much those athletes earn. A first-round NFL draft pick pays his agent hundreds of thousands of dollars. However, a minor league hockey player produces considerably less.

Female agents like Nickole Raymond (*left*), who represents LPGA golfer Michelle Wie, are becoming more common in the world of professional sports.

The agent's income also depends on an athlete's performance—both on and off the field. If the player gets involved in controversy, the agent's income is likely to drop. For instance, a sponsor will pull out of an endorsement contract if a player violates its personal conduct clause. Both the athlete and agent lose money. Sponsors shy away from players with bad reputations, so the sponsors won't even consider endorsement deals with them. That's why agents work hard to maintain and improve each client's image.

According to the US Bureau of Labor Statistics, the industry's highest earners reside in California,

GETTING AHEAD

Once you become a sports agent, you have many ways to advance in your career. Here are some of the best ways to get ahead:

1. *Work hard to recruit clients.*
2. *Work hard to stay current about changing trends.*
3. *Work hard to serve and communicate with clients.*

Go back to school. If you began with a bachelor's or master's degree, consider going back for a master's of business management or to law school. Or, take post-graduate courses to add expertise in an area you'd like to know more about—especially business management courses.

Start your own agency. If you begin your career in a sports agency or sports management company, strike out on your own. You'll need enough money to survive months with no income. And it helps if you already have your own clients to bring along.

Specialize in just one aspect of the industry. Perhaps you only negotiate contracts or perform marketing and public relations services where you place clients in special events, acting roles, and other activities that boost their image and reputation.

Texas, and the Northeast. The lowest earners live in the Southeast or Pacific Northwest. Differences in regional earnings may reflect the number, prestige, and financial status of sports teams in different areas.

SURVIVE AND ADVANCE

To survive as a sports agent, you can never sit back and relax. You must always be on the hunt for new clients. The business is full of setbacks. Clients leave for other agents, suffer career-ending injuries, or simply play out their usefulness to teams. Although many agents help clients move on to post-pro careers, all agents need to invest in new athletes at various levels of their sports. The best place to find them is by attending games and such events as the NFL combine or baseball showcase events and tournaments. That means the need for travel, travel, travel never ends.

You must always keep your credentials current and pay appropriate league fees on time to stay an active agent. Serving present clients well is critical in all areas of the business: contracts, income-producing activities, image protection, and long-term career progression, including post-sports occupations. Stay in touch with each one through constant communication, at least two or three times a week. For international clients, that means being available twenty-four hours, seven days a week in global time zones. The same goes for contact with high school, college, and professional coaches and managers, as well as

Constant networking with athletes, coaches, and team personnel is essential for sports agents. Connections often develop into business contacts as well as close personal friendships.

other team officials—even if it's just so they hear your voice from time to time.

Network. Network. Network. As you network, foster personal relationships with as many individuals in the sports realm as you can. Get to know their families. Find out what is most important to them as a lifetime philosophy. Learn their favorite cars and vacation spots. Know what they eat for breakfast. These activities help develop close ties. They also help in linking athletes and corporations for endorsement and advertising opportunities.

Diversify. Avoid relying on one or two top players for your livelihood. Involve yourself with many athletes in different sports and on different teams. Or, represent several players in the same league or sport.

Stay on top of developments in different sports as well as trends and new laws. Also, keep track of up-and-coming young athletes and keep a wish list of future clients. If you can sign a top-earning athlete, celebrate. However, don't overlook role players as you hope for a star. You can make the same amount of money representing several lower-paid athletes as you can with one superstar.

You'll need to find a way to deal with the stress the job creates. Take time for yourself through exercise or meditation. And spend time with your friends and family whenever you can.

Most important, develop and maintain a reputation as a fair negotiator as well as a person with integrity. Charges of recruiting violations, improper gifts to amateur players, making promises impossible or illegal to keep, or gambling violations have occurred in the hope of signing clients. However, an honest sports agent can make a living without playing to win at any cost.

COLLEGE AND UNIVERSITY SPORTS AGENT PROGRAMS

Indiana University
107 South Indiana Avenue
Bloomington, IN 47405
(812) 855-4848
https://www.indiana.edu
Program of study: Sport marketing and management

Louisiana State University
Office of Academic Affairs
156 Thomas Boyd Hall
Baton Rouge, LA 70803
(225) 578-3202
http://www.lsu.edu
Programs of study: Sports administration—sport leadership/sport commerce

New York University
383 Lafayette Street, 1st Floor
New York, NY 10003
(212) 998-1212
https://www.nyu.edu
Programs of study: Event management, organizational management, sports law, and sports media

North Carolina State University at Raleigh
203 Peele Hall, Campus Box 7103
Raleigh, NC 27695
(919) 515-2011
https://www.ncsu.edu
Program of study: Sport management

St. Thomas University
16401 NW 37th Avenue
Miami Gardens, FL 33054
(305) 625-6000
http://www.stu.edu
Program of study: Sports administration

Texas A & M University
Administration Building
400 Bizzell Street
College Station, TX 77843
(979) 845-3211
Program of study: Sport management

University of Florida
PO Box 117001
Gainesville, FL 32611 (352) 392-3261
http://www.ufl.edu
Program of study: Sport management

University of Georgia
210 South Jackson Street
Athens, GA 30602
(706) 542-3000
http://www.uga.edu
Program of study: Sport management

University of Kansas
1450 Jayhawk Boulevard
Lawrence, KS 66045
(785) 864-2700
https://www.ku.edu
Program of study: Sport management

University of Michigan
500 S State Street
Ann Arbor, MI 48109
(734) 764-1817
https://www.umich.edu
Program of study: Sport management

University of Minnesota Twin Cities
240 Williamson Hall
231 Pillsbury Drive SE
Minneapolis, MN 55455
(612) 625-5000

https://twin-cities.umn.edu

Program of study: Sport management

University of Oregon

1585 East 13th Avenue

Eugene, OR 97403

(541) 346-1000

http://uoregon.edu

Program of study: Business administration/concentration in sports business

Xavier University

3800 Victory Parkway

Cincinnati, OH 45207

(513) 745-3000

http://www.xavier.edu

Programs of study: Sport management, sport marketing

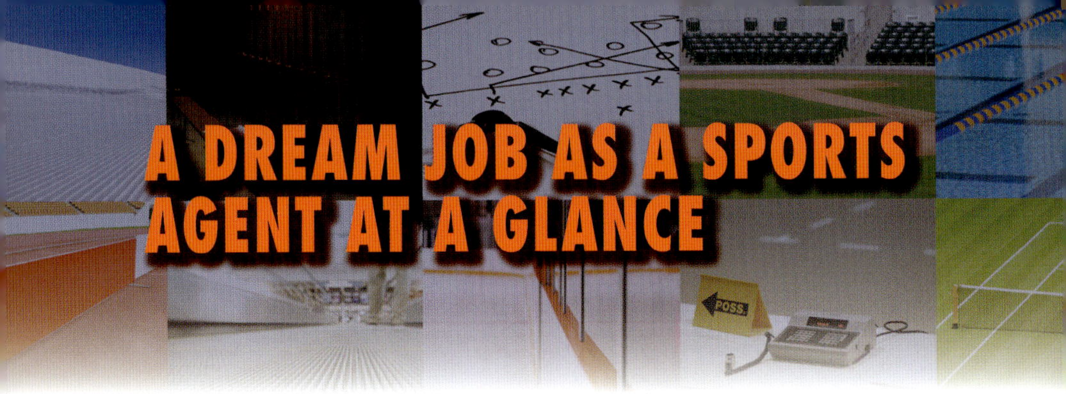

A DREAM JOB AS A SPORTS AGENT AT A GLANCE

SPORTS AGENTS

ACADEMICS

Bachelor's degree
Master's degree or law school
Internship
Certification

EXPERIENCE

Volunteer opportunities with sports teams
Employment in sports-related fields

CAREER PATHS

Employment in a sports agency
Freelance employment
Self-employment in own agency

RESPONSIBILITIES

Recruit clients

Negotiate player contracts

Arrange endorsements and personal appearances

Manage and advise clients on financial matters

Protect each client's image and reputation

Help clients plan for careers after pro athletic careers end

BUREAU OF LABOR STATISTICS INFORMATION

The Bureau of Labor Statistics (BLS) has not developed detailed occupational information for the category "Agents and Business Managers of Artists, Performers, and Athletes." However, the BLS does report that sports agents represent and promote athletes in dealings with current or prospective employers. The agents may also handle contract negotiation and other business matters for clients.

Required education for the career includes a bachelor's degree and up to five years of experience in a related field. There usually is no on-the-job training. The states of California, New York, Florida, Tennessee, and Texas have the highest number of persons employed in the category.

The BLS average mean wage for the category is nearly twice the average for all occupations. The agency expects the number of persons employed in the field to rise from 19,700 in 2014 to 20,200 by 2024, an increase of 500 new jobs. These numbers represent a projected growth rate of 3 percent, which is slower than the average for all occupations.

GLOSSARY

accounting A systematic way to keep track of financial records of a person or business.

asset Something of value that can benefit the owner in the future and that can be measured in dollars.

charisma A hard-to-define quality of charm, enthusiasm, and personal magnetism that draws others to an individual.

civil lawsuit A court case between or among two or more individuals, businesses, governments, or other entities. Typically, the person who sues seeks to recover money, not punish or imprison the other party.

cold call An unsolicited contact in an effort to sell something.

discrete mathematics A course of study that includes graph theory, counting, and social decision making, along with applications in business, planning, and management.

entrepreneurship The process of coming up with an idea, taking risks, and starting and managing a new business.

flat fee A set amount charged for a service, no matter how much work or time is involved.

freelance worker An individual who works independently on a self-employed basis.

information interview A conversation with a professional to learn about a field of employment and current job market.

integrity A personal trait that involves a combination of honesty and strong moral principles.

intermediary In professional soccer, a person who represents players in the Fédération Internationale de Football Association (FIFA), the international governing body for soccer.

kinesiology The scientific study of the anatomy and mechanics of human movement.

liability A person's or company's financial obligations owed to another person or company.

mudding a baseball Major League Baseball's practice of rubbing new baseballs to be used in games with Lena Blackburne Original Baseball Rubbing Mud to make them easier to grip.

multitasking Handling many jobs or tasks all at the same time.

net worth The total value of assets minus the amount of liabilities of a person or business.

NFL Scouting Combine A showcase event for athletes hoping to play in the National Football League.

résumé A document that lists a person's education, work experience, and activities.

risk assessment A process that identifies potential future events that could pose danger to a person or business, including measuring the likelihood and severity of those events.

risk management The process of taking measures to avoid risks or reduce their negative effects.

shuttle drill A football drill performed at the NFL combine that helps scouts, coaches, and agents evaluate players' quickness and ability to change direction.

slander A false spoken statement that harms another person's reputation.

surety bond A three-party contract between an agent, an athlete, and a surety company. The bond protects clients from any illegal or unethical actions on the agent's part. The surety company covers any resulting losses.

FOR MORE INFORMATION

Black Sports Agents Association (BSAA)

9255 West Sunset Boulevard, # 1120

West Hollywood, CA 90069-3309

(310) 858-6565

Website: http://www.blacksportsagents.com

Facebook: @blacksportagent

BSSA is an association of several hundred African American sports agents. It was founded to provide African American professional athletes with balanced representation. It also seeks to aid its members' success on the business side of professional sports.

Canadian Football League Players Association

175 Barton Street East

Stoney Creek, ON L8E-2K3

Canada

(800) 616-6865

Website: https://cflpa.com

Facebook: @CFLPA

Twitter: @CFLPA

Instagram: @CFLPA

The Canadian Football League Players Association represents players in the Canadian Football League.

conditions. It negotiates for the players on such topics as pension plan, preseason and postseason pay, and the contents of the Standard Player's Contract.

National Basketball Players Association

1133 Avenue of Americas

New York, NY 10036

(800) 955-6272

Website: http://nbpa.com

Twitter: @thenbpa

The National Basketball Players Association is the union for current professional basketball players in the National Basketball Association. Its mission is to protect the rights of players through collective bargaining, prosecuting grievances, and giving advice to players about educational opportunities.

National Football League Players Association

1133 20th Street NW, Ste. 600

Washington, DC 20036

(800) 372-2000

Website: https://www.nflpa.com

Facebook: @NFLPA

Twitter: @NFLPA

Instagram: #NFLPA

The National Football League Players Association is the players' union for the NFL. It represents players concerning their rights as well as wages, hours, and working conditions. It also assists charitable and community organizations.

National Hockey League Players' Association

20 Bay Street, Suite 1700

Toronto, ON M5J 2N8

Canada

Website: http://www.nhlpa.com

Facebook: @nhlpa

Twitter: @nhlpa

Instagram: @nhlpa_official

The National Hockey League Players' Association is the union for active players in the National Hockey League (NHL). It represents players in contract negotiations.

North American Society for Sports Management (NASSM)

NASSM Business Office

135 Winterwood Drive

Butler, PA 16001

(724)-82-6277

Website: https://www.nassm.com

Twitter: @nassm_sportmgt

NASSM supports professionals working in the fields of sport, leisure, and recreation. It encourages and supports research and such professional development topics as sport marketing, sport and the law, conflict resolution, and more.

Sport Marketing Association (SMA)

1972 Clark Avenue

Alliance, OH 44601

(330) 829-8207

Website: http://www.sportmarketingassociation.com

Facebook: @SportMarketingAssociation

Twitter: @SMA_National

SMA is an academic organization focused on sports marketing. Its members include practitioners, university professors, and students. Its annual conference includes a career fair where students can network with industry professionals.

The Sports Lawyers Association

11130 Sunrise Valley Drive, Suite 350

Reston, VA 20191

(703) 437-4377

Website: https://www.sportslaw.org/about/history.cfm

Facebook: @Sports Lawyers Association

Twitter: @sportslawyers

The Sports Lawyers Association is a nonprofit, international, professional organization of practicing lawyers, law educators, law students, and other professionals with an interest in law relating to professional and amateur sports. Its mission includes education concerning sports law.

WEBSITES

Because of the changing nature of internet links, Rosen Publishing has developed an online list of websites related to the subject of this book. This site is updated regularly. Please use this link to access the list:

http://www.rosenlinks.com/GCSI/Agent

FOR FURTHER READING

Anonymous. *The Secret Agent: Inside the World of the Football Agent*. Edinburgh, Scotland, UK: Arena Sports, 2014.

Argovitz, Jerry. *Super Agent: The One Book the NFL and NCAA Don't Want You to Read*. New York, NY: Sports Publishing, 2013.

Bacon, John U. *Fourth and Long: The Fight for the Soul of College Football*. New York, NY: Simon & Schuster, 2013.

Benedict, Jeff, and Armen Keteyian. *The System: The Glory and Scandal of Big-Time College Football*. New York, NY: Doubleday, 2013.

Carfagna, Peter. *Representing the Professional Athlete*. St. Paul, MN: West Academic Publishing, 2013.

Cindrich, Ralph. *NFL Brawler: A Player-Turned-Agent's Forty Years in the Bloody Trenches of the National Football League*. Guilford, CT: Lyons Press, 2015.

Cuban, Mark. *How to Win at the Sport of Business*. New York, NY: Diversion Publishing, 2013.

Dosh, Kristi. *Saturday Millionaires: How Winning Football Builds Winning Colleges*. New York, NY: Wiley, 2013.

Fisher, Roger, and William Ury. *Getting to Yes*. New York, NY: Random House Business Books, 2012.

Fraga, Paul. *The Art of Being a Soccer Agent: Keys to Excelling in a Fascinating Profession.* CreateSpace, 2014.

Futterman, Matthew. *Players: The Story of How Sports Became a Business.* New York, NY: Simon & Schuster, 2017.

Futterman, Matthew. *Players: The Story of Sports and Money, and the Visionaries Who Fought to Create a Revolution.* New York, NY: Simon & Schuster, 2016.

Gaul, Gilbert M. *Billion-Dollar Ball: A Journey Through the Big-Money Culture of College Football.* New York, NY: Viking, 2015.

Heitner, Darren. *How to Play the Game: What Every Sports Attorney Needs to Know.* Chicago, IL: ABA Book Publishing, 2014.

Hunt, Justin Richard. *From Mascot to Agent and Everything in Between: Career Guidance from 11 Sports Executives I Met During My Journey into Sports.* Columbus, OH: J. H. Strategists LLC, 2016.

Magowan, Kelly. *The Busy Women's Guide to...Salary Negotiation.* Melbourne, Australia: Magowan Nominees, 2015.

Nocera, Joe, and Ben Strauss. *Indentured: The Inside Story of the Rebellion Against the NCAA.* New York, NY: Portfolio, 2016.

Shropshire, Kenneth L., Timothy Davis, and N. Jeremi Duru. *The Business of Sports Agents.* Philadelphia, PA: University of Pennsylvania Press, 2016.

Steinberg, Leigh, and Michael Arkush. *The Agent: My 40-Year Career Making Deals and Changing the Game.* New York, NY: St. Martin's Griffin, 2015.

Suarez, Elizabeth. *The Art of Getting Everything: How to Negotiate for What You Want and More.* New York, NY: Morgan James Publishing, 2017.

Yate, Martin John. *Knock 'em Dead: The Ultimate Job Search Guide.* Avon, MA: Adams Media, 2017.

Zirin, Dave. *Bad Sports: How Owners Are Ruining the Games We Love.* New York, NY: The New Press, 2012.

Zirin, Dave. *Game Over: How Politics Has Turned the Sports World Upside Down.* New York, NY: The New Press, 2013.

BIBLIOGRAPHY

Allen, Scott. "Show Them the Money: 8 Famous and Infamous Sports Agents." Mental Floss.com. Retrieved March 9, 2017. http://mentalfloss.com/article/26659/show-them-money-8-famous-and-infamous-sports-agents.

American Institute of CPAs. "This Way to CPA." 2017. http://www.aicpa.org/BECOMEACPA/GETTINGSTARTED/Pages/default.aspx.

Associated Press. "Rory McIlroy Pays Whopping $20M Settlement to Ex-Agents." *New York Post*, February 4, 2015. http://nypost.com/2015/02/.../rory-mcilroys-lawsuit-settles-quickly-former-agents-celebrate.

Become-a-Sports-Agent.com. "Sports Agent Salary." 2017. http://www.become-a-sports-agent.com/salary.asp.

Belzer, Jason. "The World's Most Powerful Sports Agents 2016." *Forbes,* September 21, 2016. https://www.forbes.com/sites/jasonbelzer/2016/09/21/the-worlds-most-powerful-sports-agents-2016/#571f55ae3f73.

Berman, Zach. "A Day in the Life of an NFL Agent." *Inquirer*, May 8, 2012. http://www.philly.com/philly/sports/eagles/20120506_A_day_in_the_life_of_NFL_agent_Ed_Wasielewski.html.

Bonser, Kevin. "How the NFL Draft Works." How Stuff Works. Retrieved March 2, 2017. http://entertainment.howstuffworks.com/nfl-draft.htm.

Bradshaw, D'Bria. "Revisions to the Uniform Athlete Agents Act." Sports Agent Blog, July 20, 2015. http://sportsagentblog.com/2015/07/20/revisions-to-the-uniform-athlete-agents-act.

Bureau of Labor Statistics. "Occupational Employment and Wages, May 2015: 13-1011 Agents and Business Managers of Artists, Performers, and Athletes." March 30, 2016. https://www.bls.gov/oes/current/oes131011.htm.

Canter, David. "Confessions of...a Sports Agent." ESPN.com. Retrieved January 18, 2017. http://www.espn.com/page2/s/confessions/agent.html.

College Foundation of North Carolina. "Sports Agent Interviews Insider Info." Retrieved March 8, 2017. https://www1.cfnc.org/Plan/For_A_Career/Career_Profile/Career_Profile.aspx?id=UTiLg1DaID4NJwz4lMpiYwXAP3DPAXXAP3DPAX&screen=9.

College Foundation of North Carolina. "Sports Agent What They Do." 2017. https://www1.cfnc.org/Plan/For_A_Career/Career_Profile/Career_Profile.aspx?id=UTiLg1DaID4NJwz4lMpiYwXAP3DPAXXAP3DPAX.

Gaines, Cork. "NBA Players Have the Highest-Average Salaries in the World but No League Spends More on Players than the NFL." *Business Insider*, November 14, 2016. http://www.businessinsider.com/nfl-mlb-nba-nhl-average-sports-salaries-2016-11.

Gentile, Marie. "The Average Sports Agent's Commission." *Houston Chronicle*, 2017. http://work.chron.com/average-sports-agents-commission-21083.html.

Grossman, Ron. "90 Years Ago: Red Grange's Amazing Game." *Chicago Tribune*, October 10, 2015. http://

www.chicagotribune.com/news/history/ct-red-grange-flashback-1012-20141012-story.html.

Heitner, Darren. "Football Agent's Lawsuit Against Former Agency Asks Court to Void Parts of Employment Agreement." *Forbes*, May 12, 2013. https://www.forbes.com/sites/darrenheitner/2013/05/12/football-agents-lawsuit-against-former-agency-asks-court-to-void-parts-of-employment-agreement/#2bed53db7b25.

Heitner, Darren. "Football Agents Sued by Recruiter for Not Paying Him Off." Sports Agent Blog, November 5, 2015. http://sportsagentblog.com/2015/11/05/football-agents-sued-by-recruiter-for-not-paying-him-off.

Heitner, Darren. "Roc Nation Sports Sued for Stealing Melvin Ingram from Agent." *Forbes*, November 3, 2016. https://www.forbes.com/sites/darrenheitner/2016/11/03/roc-nation-sports-sued-for-stealing-melvin-ingram-from-agent/#12d4ee361fce.

Kelchner, Luanne. "Top Ten Effective Negotiation Skills." *Houston Chronicle*, 2017. http://smallbusiness.chron.com/top-ten-effective-negotiation-skills-31534.html.

Major League Baseball Players Association. "Frequently Asked Questions." Retrieved January 18, 2017. http://www.nmnathletics.com/ViewArticle.dbml?&DB_OEM_ID=34000&ATCLID=211044889#intern.

My Job Search. "Sports Agent Jobs." 2017. https://myjobsearch.com/careers/sports-agent.html.

National Basketball Association. "Becoming an Agent." Retrieved January 15, 2017. http://nbpa.com/becoming-an-agent.

National Football League. "How to Become an Agent." Retrieved January 15, 2017. https://www.nflpa.com.

National Hockey League Players' Association. "Certified Player Agents." Retrieved January 15, 2017. http://www.nhlpa.com/inside-nhlpa/certified-player-agents.

Nazar, Jason. "The 21 Principles of Persuasion." *Forbes*, March 26, 2013. https://www.forbes.com/sites/jasonnazar/2013/03/26/the-21-principles-of-persuasion/#6926b700a4c9.

Rudulph, Heather Wood. "Get That Life: How I Became an NFL Agent." *Cosmopolitan*, March 7, 2016. http://www.cosmopolitan.com/career/a53840/nfl-agent-kelli-masters-get-that-life.

Sabitano, Colleen. "How to Network in Your Academic Department." Internships.com, 2017. http://www.internships.com/student/resources/prep/how-to-network-in-your-academic-department.

Solomon, Jon. "D. J. Fluker/Luther Davis story Has Legal Questions Over Alabama Sports Agent Laws." Yahoo Sports, September 12, 2013. http://www.al.com/sports/index.ssf/2013/09/yahoo_story_on_dj_flukerluther.html.

Sports Management Degree Guide. "What Does a Sports Agent Do?" 2016. http://www.sports-management-degrees.com/faq/what-does-a-sports-agent-do.

Sports Management Degree Hub. "Show Me the Money: So…You Want to Be a Sports Agent?" 2015. http://www.sportsmanagementdegreehub.com/sports-agent.

Sports Management Degree Hub. "6 Places to Find Sports Management Internships." December 26, 2013. http://www.sportsmanagementdegreehub.com/sports-management-internships.

USA Soccer. "FIFA Regulations on Working with Intermediaries." 2017. http://www.ussoccer.com/about/federation-services/intermediaries.

USLegal.com. "The Sports Agent Responsibility and Trust Act." Retrieved March 8, 2017. https://sportslaw.uslegal.com/the-sports-agent-responsibility-and-trust-act.

USLegal.com. "Uniform Athlete Agent Act Law and Legal Definition." Retrieved March 8, 2017. https://definitions.uslegal.com/u/uniform-athlete-agent-act.

WorkInSports.com. "Make Your Passion Your Career." Retrieved March 7, 2017. https://www.workinsports.com/sports-jobs.asp.

INDEX

T

U

V

W

ABOUT THE AUTHOR

Mary-Lane Kamberg is a professional writer who has written about college and professional sports in *America's Most Winning Teams: North Carolina Basketball*, *A Career As an Athletic Trainer*, and *The Vision*. She has also written sports articles for *Swimming World*, *Current Health*, the *Kansas City Star*, and *KC Sports and Fitness*. She is a former swimming coach for the Kansas City Blazers swim team.

PHOTO CREDITS

Cover, p. 1 Allstars/Shutterstock.com; cover, p. 1 (background) Eric Broder Van Dyke/Shutterstock.com; pp. 4-5 Rena Schild/Shutterstock.com; p. 9 Jeff Golden/Getty Images; p. 11 Dave Sandford/National Hockey League/Getty Images; p. 13 George Doyle/Stockbyte/Thinkstock; pp. 16-17 Petr Toman/Shutterstock.com; p. 22 Bettmann/Getty Images; pp. 26-27 Dmitry Serebryakov/TASS/Getty Images; pp. 28-29 Geoff Caddick/AFP/Getty Images; p. 34 Blend Images-Hill Street Studios/Brand X Pictures/Getty Images; pp. 36-37 Doug Pensinger/Getty Images; pp. 40-41 Michael Zagaris/Getty Images; p. 43 Monkeybusinessimages/iStock/Thinkstock; p. 44 Andrey Popov/Shutterstock.com; p. 47 Dragon Images/Shuterstock.com; pp. 50-51 Iakov Filimonov/Shutterstock.com; pp. 54-55 AGIF/Shutterstock.com; p. 59 Digital Vision/Photodisc/Thinkstock; p. 61 Aspen Photo/Shutterstock.com; p. 64 Piskel/iStock/Thinkstock; pp. 68-69 Vlad Teodor/Shutterstock.com; pp. 70-71 Stuart Jenner/Shutterstock.com; p. 75 Icon Sportswire/Getty Images; p. 77 LuckyImages/Shutterstock.com; pp. 80-81 Thearon W. Henderson/Getty Images; pp. 84-85 Andrew Redington/Getty Images; p. 88 The Washington Post/Getty Images; p. 91 Keeton Gale/Shutterstock.com; p. 92 Ken Wolter/Shutterstock.com; p. 97 Doug Benc/Getty Images; pp. 100-101 Shironosov/iStock/Thinkstock; interior design elements: © www.istockphoto.com/ hudiemm (grid pattern); http://lostandtaken.com (striped border); pp. 8, 25, 42, 58, 74, 90, 103, 106, 108, 109, 112, 116, 119, 124 (montage) © www.iStockphoto.com, Shutterstock.com.

Design: Brian Garvey; Layout: Ellina Litmanovich;
Editor: Bethany Bryan; Photo Researcher: Sherri Jackson